Frugal Living Tips To Save You Money

Cynthia Thomas

Copyright © 2012 Cynthia Thomas

All Rights Reserved.

ISBN-13: 978-1480038530

Contents

Frugal Living Tips to Save You Money! 1

It's a Family Affair! 2

The Credit Card Trap 3

Baby Steps that Save Money 4

Frugal Tips 6

Baking Soda - Miracle "One for Everything" Powder! 19

Baking Powder Tips and Hints 20

Frugal Living Tips to Save You Money!

There's an old saying, "There's more than one way to skin a cat," that I have heard during my life and while growing up. By the same token, there's more than one way to save money, and not having to do without. Everyone can save money somehow.

Little steps can make a world of difference. There are countless ways to trim your budget, yet still live nicely. Making minor changes and substitutions can make a huge difference in the amount of money that goes out of your house monthly. Bank those savings for a rainy day or a special something you've been wanting.

It's a Family Affair!

Frugal living is a family affair, not just a one person thing. Get everyone involved that lives in your household. It won't happen overnight, but very soon you will begin to see the difference in your bills, your savings, your stress level.

So get everyone in the home involved in living the frugal life! Teach them to reuse, not throw everything out. Get them involved in not wasting. Teach the kids how to save part of their allowance, and the value of a dollar.

The Credit Card Trap

In today's world, too many people try to live on money they don't even have, using credit cards for instance. Why put yourself into such debt when you can make it fine on the income you have coming in? For those that feel they must have credit cards to live, look for cards that have lower interest rates. Close out those high interest rate cards. Are you paying a monthly fee just to have a card? This will eat at your pocketbook in a heartbeat.

At one time, I was paying more than $9.00 a month just to have a credit card. When I finally wised up and added it up, I was paying this credit card company almost $80 a year just to use this card! While I must admit I liked the idea of having credit cards, the one thing I never counted on happened.

In a day's time, circumstances happened that left me unable to pay my bills. When the late fees starting getting added along with the high interest rates, and monthly fees on some cards, I soon was way in over my head. It was not long before over the line fees were also being added.

Baby Steps that Save Money

One mistake a person makes, in trying to change their spending habits, is to attempt to change everything at once. While that is an admirable thought, it's not realistic. Pick one or two areas and start, such as cutting back on eating out or credit card spending. As you get one thing under control, move on to other areas, such as couponing and food buying. In no time, you'll be living the frugal life, have much less stress, and be happier!

A good way to find out how much money you are spending on groceries and nonfat items, gas, fast food, dining out, and other items, is to keep the receipts for one month on everything you spend money on. After that a month is up, bring the receipts out and add up the amount for all unnecessary items. How much money could you have saved?

Take that idea a step further, and starting keeping up with how much you are saving by being frugal and using sales, coupons, thrift stores, combining trips to save gas, and reusing items. After a month of living this way, add up those amounts and see how much you have saved verses what you would have spent.

Add the two months together, and you most likely will be very surprised to learn how much money you actually spend unnecessarily. Now add in this amount the total you pay out to credit card companies every month. Those are also unnecessary expenses. Yes, you CAN live without credit cards! Is the amount you can save a month getting higher? Do you like the amount of money you can save? With that money you save, you can pay cash for the things you would have charged on credit cards, take a vacation paid for in cash, and without a bill coming in for it the next month.

The following tips are but the tip of the iceberg on ways to save you money every month. Remember the days of old when families lived on so much less than what we do today? They survived just fine without two or three vehicles, without credit cards, without a two-income family, without a high priced mortgage, without expensive clothing, without their children owning the toy store, and without most everything that we today take for granted. We CAN do it today also!

Frugal Tips

At the end of the day, put your change into a jar to save. Then hide it from yourself. You will find that this can add up to a substantial amount quickly. Call this your "Saving For A Rainy Day Savings." It's a great way to save for a vacation, gifts, etc.

1. By far the easier way to save money in any house is to simply turn off the lights that are not being used. When you leave a room, even if you are going back, turn off the lights as you leave out.

2. Are you watching TV? If not, why is it on? Turn it off unless someone is watching it! I have had friends that actually leave their home to go to town, and leave their lights and TV running. Ever little bit helps!

3. Before making ANY special purchase, no matter how small the cost, think about it first. Do you REALLY need this item? Is it worth the money? Is there any other way I can do the same thing this item will, without spending this amount of money on it? Impulse buying can quickly eat into your savings, so always think before you buy.

4. Disposable diapers are nice, but they run into a lot of expense. Use cloth diapers at home in the day, and save the disposable ones for going places and night time. With the average cost for a package of disposable diapers, you can save a good deal of money in the two year's baby is in diapers.

5. After Baby has passed the first baby food stages, feed Baby what the rest of the family eats. You can grind or mush foods for Baby. Remember - nothing spicy! Babies can eat veggies, fruits, and a lot that you prepare at home for a fraction of the cost.

6. Buy clothes at yard sales or second hand for the baby or small child. As fast as babies and toddlers grow, why buy new clothes they won't even wear out before they've outgrown them? I have found practically brand new clothes for pennies in this way.

7. Don't spend the money on small trash bags. Save the ones you get from the grocery store. They work well and are free, and hold trash just as well as those store-bought ones. If you shop different stores, you can even get different colored ones.

8. Save on your power bill in the summer by cooking early in the morning and late at night, having only to heat foods up during the day. The less you can use the oven during the hottest part of the summer, the better on your finances.

9. Use a clothes line to dry your clothes. If no clothes line is available, only run your dryer early in the morning or late at night, to keep from heating up the house even more. The heat these two appliances put off will make your air units run more, so using them during the coolest times possible will help a lot.

10. The opposite is true for the winter months. Cooking, using the oven, and drying clothes during the coldest part of the winter can help keep your heating costs lower. Since you have to cook anyway, why not let the heat of the stove help heat the home at the same time?

11. Use your dryer sheets more than once. I use mine three times or more, and they still work just as well. This saves money, and your clothes are just as soft and static free.

12. Learn to do basic mending. Don't throw away a piece of clothing just because it has a hem undone, a hole, or lost button. The price of clothing has become so ridiculously high that one wonders how anyone can afford to throw something out just because it needs a tiny bit of mending.

13. Most have heard the old saying, "Waste not, want not." Save leftovers and have later, rather than throw them out. Pass on outgrown clothing to other children or thrift stores. Don't just leave the water running if not in use.

14. Turn off the lights when no one needs them. Don't make unnecessary trips, and save on gas. If something can be used again, use it again.

15. Buy your holiday items on clearance the day after a major holiday and save them until the next year. For example, I often find Christmas wrapping paper and decorations at about 75% off the retail price the two days after Christmas.

16. If you enjoy sewing, or are interested in learning how, you can save tons of money on blankets. Use those old clothes that have become worn, cut them into patterns, and make a quilt! Besides saving money, these quilts make a wonderful heirloom, and bring back fond memories. Save old shirt sleeves and pants legs from alterations for the quilt also.

17. Don't buy rags from a store just to use them as rags. Cut those worn towels and hand towels into smaller pieces. These are wonderful for dish rags, dusting rags, bathroom cleaning rags, and washing the vehicle.

18. Buttons on old clothing can be reused again and again. They can be sewn onto new clothes, used for counting practice for small children, and used for various craft projects.

19. Kids have holes in the knees of their pants? What kid doesn't sooner or later? Don't throw the pants out, make the pants into shorts or sew colorful patches over both knees. This adds more life to the piece of clothing.

20. You can save at least $10 per head if you cut hair at home. I save $30 a month by cutting hair at home. I paid $25 for a home barber set, which paid for itself the first month. No, the kids don't have the latest fad haircut, but they are nice looking and look cool too.

21. Are you paying too much for your prescription medicines? Try getting a generic brand next time. Every generic medicine I have ever used is just as good as the nationally known brand, but costs much less. For those that need a lot of different medications on a regular basis, the cost can run into a hefty amount.

22. Prepare meals at home. Eating out gobbles up your money! Buy foods that you have to cook, rather than already boxed or made. Save the boxed and frozen meals to make on those sick days or when you absolutely cannot cook a meal. Set yourself up a time to eat out, once a week, once a month, or just when you are gone all day and must eat out. Make eating

out a special occasion, not something you do just because you don't want to cook.

23. Don't shop for groceries when you're hungry. You end up buying more than you intended. Make a grocery list before leaving the house. Then stick to it! If you must buy name brand items, search for items you have coupons for or that are on sale. You can save more if your store has double and triple coupon days. Sales and coupons combined with a prepared shopping list adds up to great savings.

24. Eat less meat at a meal. Use "stretcher" meats like ground beef, tuna, and chicken. Cook the meal with the meat added into something else, such as you own made at home "Help that Hamburger Out" concoction, soups, or stews.

25. Rent a video rather than go out to the movies. If you'd rather go to the movies, check out the theater's bargain time and day. Resist the urge to buy the expensive popcorn, candy, and drinks. We used to sneak our drinks and snacks in. It saved us tons of money!

26. Going out for the day and need a cooler for drinks or food? Use your own ice, rather than buying a bag or two of it. The day before start emptying up those ice trays into a container. It's an easy way to save yourself a couple of bucks.

27. Stop smoking! Besides the obvious health reasons, this will save you tons of money. Don't burn up your money in cigarettes, but rather put that money to good use. The amount you save in just one month will astound you.

28. Do you have a garden? Don't spend money on a watering can! Save those cans your coffee or veggies come in. After washing them, use an ice pick or other sharp object and poke a few small holes in the bottom of the can. You've got a free instant watering can.

29. Brush those teeth! It'll save you a shocking amount in dental costs. Call it preventive maintenance. Remember to replace that toothbrush about every four months. Even though it might not appear to need it, follow the dentist's instructions. Teeth are hard to replace once they are lost to poor care.

30. Do you really HAVE to have makeup? You're beautiful without it! Show the world the real you and save money too. At the very least, have some makeup-free days.

31. Turn off the water when it's not being used. When brushing teeth, don't just let it run. When washing dishes turn it off between rinses. Use the cold water setting on washing clothes unless they are really dirty. Rinse clothes in cold water, not warm or hot.

32. When washing clothes, make sure you have a full load. The washer uses the same amount of electricity on a full load as it does as partial load. Fill that tub up!

33. Check the air in your tires. Tires that are under inflated use more gas. It also makes for a smoother ride. Roll those windows up for less air drag on the vehicle. This will save you more gas.

34. Consolidate your trips. Don't go to town today to shop, and then turn around and go back tomorrow to shop again. Get everything you need to do taken care

of in one trip. Save that gas, it's not getting any cheaper.

35. Save plastic bowls. Bowls that you buy containing margarine, yogurt, and cottage cheese can be used to store foods in. They work great in the freezer also.

36. When you buy jelly or jam in a glass container, save the container to use for a drinking glass. If you buy four or six of the same thing at the same time, you have a matching set of drinking glasses, all for the price of the jelly or jam.

37. If you are looking to decorate your walls, you don't have to spend a small fortune to do it. Look at the garage and yard sales, thrift stores, and second hand shops for nice used decorations. You might find a great deal on something that just needs to be cleaned. Also, an old calendar with pictures makes excellent wall pictures. Spend a dollar at the store on a cheap frame and place the picture in it. Better yet, find a frame at a yard sale for a quarter!

38. Are you washing your hard earned money down the drain with soaps and shampoos? Buy the generic or cheaper brand! It cleans just as well as the five dollars a bottle kind. How many times have the kids left the soap in the tub, only for you to discover it later melted away to a gooey glob? Try cheap store brand liquid soap! Yes, they might squirt too much out until they get the hang of it. What I do is save an empty bottle, and put a small amount in it so they don't waste the entire bottle.

39. Use a line to dry some of your clothes, such as blankets, spreads, sheets. Save the dryer for clothes

you'd rather have softer. No room for a line? Let clothes dry for about 20 minutes in the dryer, then remove them and put on hangers. Hang the clothes on your shower curtain rail to finish air drying. Use a line to dry some of your clothes, such as blankets, spreads, sheets. Save the dryer for clothes you'd rather have softer. No room for a line? Let clothes dry for about 20 minutes in the dryer, then remove them and put on hangers. Hang the clothes on your shower curtain rail to finish air drying.

40. Use a line to dry some of your clothes, such as blankets, spreads, sheets. Save the dryer for clothes you'd rather have softer. No room for a line? Let clothes dry for about 20 minutes in the dryer, then remove them and put on hangers. Hang the clothes on your shower curtain rail to finish air drying.

41. If you use a dishwasher to wash your dishes, don't let it run all the way through the cycle. Once the washing is done, turn the dishwasher off and open the door to let the dishes dry. This not only saves on your power bill, it helps the dishes try quicker and with fewer spots. Turn off the heat dry cycle of your dishwasher.

42. Buy store brand bags for the freezer that you can reseal, rather than the name brand. They are about half price and work just as well. Wash them instead of throwing them away after being used, unless they've had raw meat in them.

43. Use water and vinegar in a spray bottle to clean your windows and mirrors. It's much less than the name brand window cleaner and works just as well. Some people use crumbled newspapers to clean windows. While I have not personally tried this, I am told it

works wonderfully and leaves the windows nicely cleaned.

44. Set some fans up in your house to help save on cooling costs. Ceiling fans and floor fans help to circulate the air, thus keeping the air units from running so long. Set your air controls to 78 degrees and leave it. Turning the temperature back and forth uses more electricity.

45. Is your phone bill still too high even after taking off the unnecessary phone services and using a less expensive long distance company? Cut out all the unnecessary phone services from your phone. You can say a lot of money each month, depending on how many extras you use. Look for cheaper long distance. Or have your phone services bundled and get a discount for doing so. Another idea is the use of prepaid phone cards.

46. Lower your cell phone costs by looking for cheaper cell phone service, such as Straight Talk. Do the kids really need their own cell phone? Cut out the unnecessary extras. With the price of cell phone usage, it makes sense (and cents!) to only get what you actually need and use.

47. Keeping your curtains and shades closed in the summer will help keep the heat out of your house, thereby keeping down the power bill. The window coverings help to keep the heat out and the cool in. The reverse if true for the winter months. Keep your shades and curtains open during the day and let the warm sun come into your home, helping to warm it up and saving on the heating bill.

48. Save all the little bits of leftover sausage, bacon, and ham and keep it in the freezer. These make yummy additions to omelets. They also make great additions to soups, rice, beans, noodles, and potatoes.

49. Don't buy beef tips that are already cut up for soups or stews. Buy a whole roast and cut it yourself. Besides saving money, you can precook it and freeze for a later meal.

50. Unless there is a good sale on grated cheese, don't buy it! Buy block cheese and grate it yourself. It's usually much less than the already grated kind.

51. Don't buy groceries in a convenience store. These tiny stores are usually way overpriced. Buy your groceries in a grocery store, and save yourself a heap of money.

52. Make those birthday cakes as home, even if it's a boxed mix. Bakery cakes might look nice, but they are very expensive. The same with cookies; Make them at home using a box mix or from scratch. While they look delicious, the ones you make yourself are just as good, yet cost much less.

53. In the mood for pizza? Don't call the pizza place, make your own at home! For the price of what you pay for delivery or dine in, you can feed the neighbors!

54. Learn to love those leftovers! They can be frozen for a later meal, or as an addition to soups or stews. As children, we lived on leftovers. Though there were times we thought we'd not be able to eat another

leftover meal, none of us starved. As I recall, our tummies were quite filled out.

55. Where possible, buy in bulk. Most items are less when you buy more of a product. Watch those prices, however, because this is not always the case.

56. If your faucets are dripping, it's time to replace them. The dripping itself can drive you insane. If you are on city water, you will see a change in your water bill once that leak is fixed. For those on well water, your light bill will lower, since the pump is run off electricity. Water leaks only send your power bill or water bill higher, so invest a few dollars and fix it. It'll save you money in the long run, and you can sleep better at night not hearing the dripping from the sink.

57. If you have lots of stores in your area, do some comparison shopping. When we were kids, my Mom would take a huge cooler for the cold items, and make it a day of shopping. Combine comparison shopping with coupons and sales, and you can save a lot.

58. Substitute dry milk for baking and cooking. This saves money, it's just as good as regular milk, and does not change the taste of the food. You can also save used milk containers, and mix the powered milk half and half with the regular milk. This tastes a little different from the regular milk, but the taste will grow on you. It also cuts your milk bill way down.

59. Save those aluminum cans! There are many places that buy aluminum cans. Recycling is not only good for our planet it reduces wastes, and puts some money back into your pocket.

60. Stop using that electric can opener! Grandma did just fine with the manual one, so why can't we? Save on your power bill by cutting back on the electric items used in your home.

61. Can you get to where you want to go within a reasonable amount of time walking or riding a bike? Save on gas and get exercise at the same time! Take a bike ride or a nice walk, and leave the car parked at home. Your body will love you more for taking better care of it, too.

62. If you subscribe to cable TV or have a piped in satellite TV system, cut off the subscription to the movie channels. If you must have one, keep only one. This will save you many dollars a month. Rent a video on discount night, or see a movie at the theater on discount night. Turn off all those extra cable, Dish, and DirecTV movie channels and huge program packages. You can get a NetFlix subscription and still saves loads of money!

63. Change the filters at least every two months in your central air and heat units. You will use more power and spend more money leaving a dirty one in. The dirtier the filter is, the harder and longer the unit runs trying to cool or heat your home.

64. Check your windows and doors for air leakage. You're not trying to heat or cool the outside, so make sure the air is staying inside. Investing a few dollars in caulking and insulation will save a lot of money later in power costs.

65. Save on babysitting costs by trading out! The cost of child care today is extravagant. How can one afford to pay a babysitter for a night out? One thought is

trading out with other families. They babysit tonight for you for free, and you babysit a night for them free. This saves tons of money!

66. Don't buy cheap pots and pans! While this might seem to go against the frugal idea, it's an investment worthwhile. Unless you are just starting out and cannot afford good kitchen ware, it would be well worth the money to buy higher priced pots. Remember you will be cooking a lot and these pots will get a lot of use. Cheap pots and pans do not last. But look for sales on good pots before buying!

67. Shoes are another area you do not want to be frugal in. Your feet need good shoes. Look for sales on good, name brand shoes. Cheap shoes are fine for yard work, for example, but not for wearing all day. Protect those feet, they're the only two you've got.

Baking Soda - Miracle "One for Everything" Powder!

Baking soda is not just for cooking anymore! Baking Soda has fast become "THE" all purpose cleaner for just about everything imaginable. Besides its obvious cleaning abilities, it is environmentally safe, and costs much less than the average cleaner. If you want to save money while cleaning your home, consider investing in a lot of baking soda. The price you pay will save you a lot of money in the long run.

Following are but a few ideas for using baking soda. There are endless possibilities for this wonderful powder!

Baking Powder Tips and Hints

Be sure to buy the store brand of baking soda. It is the same thing and works just as well as name brand baking soda, but for a lesser price. Since you will be using a lot of baking soda, this will pay off even more. Just remember that although it may seem you are spending a lot on baking soda, you are actually saving money because you are not buying all of those expensive cleaners.

Don't buy the expensive carpet deodorizing sprinkle-on powders. To keep your carpets smelling fresh, sprinkle baking soda over the floor, and let it sit for a few minutes, then vacuum.

Are your sink drains starting to have an odor to them? Sprinkling a touch of baking soda in the sink, followed by a small amount of vinegar, will take that smell right out of the sink drains.

Use baking soda to clean your sinks! It won't scratch your finish, and it cleans just as well as those expensive cleaners, for a fraction of the cost.

Add a cup of baking soda to your laundry wash along with the regular detergent. This will help soften your water, along with freshening the clothes.

Does your refrigerator have a strange odor when you open the door? Take a small cup or bowl, put about three tablespoons of baking soda in it, and put this uncovered into the refrigerator and leave. The baking soda absorbs the odors. Change the baking soda about every couple of months. This works the same in the freezer, if you have an upright model.

Use baking soda to put grease fires. Sprinkling the baking soda over the grease fire will extinguish it.

Sprinkle a small amount of baking soda in the bottom of your garbage cans to help keep the odor down.

If you have cats, sprinkling baking soda in the litter box will help keep the odor chased away.

Does your dog have that "wet dog" smell? Try sprinkling some baking soda onto the dog's fur, then brush it out.

Try sprinkling baking soda in the bottom of your laundry hamper to help keep the dirty clothes from having a lingering odor.

Does someone in the family suffer from foot odor, thereby causing the rest of the family to suffer also? Try sprinkling a tiny amount of baking soda into the bottom of the shoes. It will help eliminate the odor.

Baking soda makes a wonderful antacid, and for pennies. Mix half a teaspoon of baking soda with about four ounces (one cup) of water, and drink. Use baking soda to clean your stove. Sprinkle baking soda over the area to be cleaned, wipe with a damp cloth.

Pet accidents can be taken care of with baking soda. If the pet has an accident, sprinkle with baking soda and let dry, then vacuum. The baking soda will take care of the stain and the odor.

Clean the inside of your drip coffee pot maker with baking soda, water, and vinegar. Fill the coffee pot with warm water from the tap, add about half a cup of vinegar to this, and about two teaspoons of baking soda. Make sure the baking soda is dissolved, and pour the mixture through the coffee maker, just as if you were going to make coffee. After this finishes, run two to three pots of plain water through the coffee maker. You have a clean and fresh coffee maker now.

Use baking soda to get burned on food off of your pots or baking dishes. Add some baking soda in the bottom of the pot or pan, add some water, and let soak for a couple of hours. The food will wipe right off without having to scrub.

Add about two tablespoons of baking soda to your dishwasher's rinsing agent area. This will stop the spots.

Got kids? Kids got crayons? Do the kids like to decorate your walls with those crayons? Mine too! After many times of needless and elbow breaking scrubbing to attempt to remove it, without much success, I found an easier way! Get a damp washcloth and dip it in baking soda. This takes the crayon markings right off, and without compromising your elbows and sanity to do it!

Heal marks on floors from shoes can easily be removed by using baking soda. Using a wet mop or towel, sprinkle baking soda on the marked area and clean as usual.

THE END

Visit my websites, FrugalMagazine.com and FrugalSimplicity.com for other ideas and information on how to live the frugal life, save money, budget, find bargains, get freebies, live on less, reuse items, be thrifty, and be happy doing it.

www.ingramcontent.com/pod-product-compliance
Lightning Source LLC
Chambersburg PA
CBHW061523180526
45171CB00001B/303